The Simplified & Sanctified Marriage

The Simplified & Sanctified Marriage

Loving God by Loving Spouse

DR. JENDAYO K. GRADY

The Simplified & Sanctified Marriage

Loving God by Loving Spouse

by Dr. Jendayo K. Grady

Printed in the United States of America

ISBN 9780986423918

Foundation House Publishing, LLC

DISCLAIMER

The insights and strategies expressed in this book may not be suitable for every situation. The author and publisher are not rendering psychological, marital, legal, or any other treatment. The author nor the publisher shall be liable for damages arising from following the strategies in this book. Furthermore, the characters and specific scenarios in this book are fictitious and are not extrapolated from the author's professional counseling or therapeutic sessions.

DEDICATION

This book is dedicated to all who are truly seeking to have a marriage that glorifies God.

ACKNOWLEDGMENTS

I want to acknowledge God for giving me the instructions, the inspiration, and the insights needed to write this book. Thank you for being the perfect model for marriage.

To my wife, Kellie for championing this work with your wisdom, encouragement, and editing. Your perspectives have made this book significantly better! Thank you for your continued love, support, and partnership with me as we strive to make our marriage simplified and sanctified.

To my parents, Paul & Carrie Grady, for being great examples to emulate. I want to be married for over 55 years just like you.

To the staff at Foundation House Publishing, LLC., thank you for the support and guidance.

To everyone who encouraged, invested in, and/or contributed to this project in any way, Thank You!

Contents

Introduction

THIS BOOK IS designed to give you a simplified understanding of God's purpose for and his process of marriage. It is not designed to be an exhaustive resource on marriage. Rather, it is a redirection or clarification of our focus to the most important purposes of ***holy matrimony.*** The most important purpose of marriage is that it is an institution created *by* God *for* his own glory. This book seeks to drive that truth deeply into our souls.

I am not writing as one who has arrived and mastered the craft; rather, I am writing as one overflowing with experiences, insights, missteps, failures, and revelation that have helped me to navigate my marital journey. Furthermore, as a clinical psychologist and pastoral counselor, I have counseled hundreds of married couples, giving me more objective insight into the issues of marriage.

I started writing a book about marriage with the intent of being deep and clever. I began to write concepts and pontifications that tickled my fancy and gave the appearance that I really knew what I was talking about. Then, I hit an iceberg, and all of a sudden, the desire, the energy, the focus, and the direction seemed to sink like the lofty Titanic.

The reason for this collision was two-fold. First, I needed to live a little longer. I needed to understand some of the principles I was writing about from more of an experiential standpoint. Sometimes, you just have to live life for a while to really understand some things. Second, God needed to change my approach. I had set a deadline to finish the book that I did not and could not meet. This was not merely writer's block. It felt like God was blocking me. One day God **K.i**.**s.s**.ed me. God was urging me to "Keep it simple son." God was urging me to simplify the approach to having a healthy and holy marriage. God did not want the book to be deep, clever, and complex. He wanted the book to be effective. Simplicity is often related to effectiveness.

We have been inundated with books, seminars, teachings, and sermons on love and marriage. Sometimes, as we endeavor to negotiate the terrain of the technical minutia of scripture and psychological material, we become overwhelmed. Now, this book is not designed to underwhelm you! To the contrary, I believe you will be positively overwhelmed with how simplistic God's will is for spouses. When truth is reduced to its simplest form, then obedience becomes a simple function of *choice* rather than a function of trying to understand confusing realities.

Some of the principles we will cover in this book may be something that you have heard before. Some will be totally new. My prayer is that this book will help you to take what you already know conceptually and experience it personally. For the new material, my hope is that it is practical enough for you to understand and apply to your personal situation. Each chapter ends with a summary of the major principles in that chapter along with a Simplified & Sanctified Exhortation (SSE), biblical passages, and a prayer for specific application. Finally, each chapter also ends with a journal page to write down applicable information that pertains to you.

I pray that as you read this book, the Holy Spirit will guide you not only to understanding, but to joyful and successful practice as well. God bless you!

Dr. Jendayo Grady

THE PREPARATION PHASE

PART I

Chapter 1

The Blueprint

For I know the plans I have for you, declares the LORD, plans for welfare and not for evil, to give you a future and a hope. (Jeremiah 29:11)[1]

THE ABILITY OF men and women to build tall, beautiful, and complex structures fascinates me. What a massive undertaking it is to get all of the materials and the

[1] English Standard Version (ESV)

laborers to be functional and fit where they belong. Sometimes it takes years to complete a building project because it requires ensuring that all of the intricate details are completed in a satisfactory manner. Some buildings are extremely tall such as the Burj Khalifa in Dubai 2,722 feet, or the CN Tower in Toronto 1,815 feet. My family and I were blessed to ride the elevator to the top of the CN tower. We were in awe of it and contemplated the work and skill that went into producing it. I was mesmerized with how high I was in the air, and how small other buildings looked from my vantage point. Some buildings were made with solar panels, and other buildings were made with the pure gold like the temple that Solomon built. All of the aforementioned buildings differed significantly in design, value, and purpose. However, what all of these and other major buildings have in common is the need for a blueprint.

A blueprint is defined as 1. *something used as a guide for building or doing something else; 2. a detailed plan.* A slight deviation from the blueprint can result in major structural and foundational problems. Similarly, marriage is a very grand and complex institution that requires strict adherence to the blueprint. The problem for many couples is they begin to build their marriage without ever consulting the blueprint.

When the blueprint is not followed precisely, it is only a matter of time before the building begins to crumble.

The architect of marriage has meticulously laid out plans in the blueprint and has guaranteed enjoyment and stability. This guarantee, however, is only applicable if we follow the specific details of the plan. Well, who is this architect? The architect is none other than Almighty God, the designer and sustainer of holy matrimony. God is the perfect architect of marriage because he created the two most important human elements in a holy marriage, man and woman. Furthermore, the glue that binds husband and wife, according to the blueprint, is love. God knows a thing or two about love because he is love! Since God created man and woman, he knows every detail about their tendencies, predispositions, needs, desires, strengths, and weaknesses. God's purpose in creating marriage fits into the larger context of his divine purpose, which is to be glorified.

God is the architect and the Holy Bible is the blueprint! The specific details of the blueprint, which describe how holy matrimony looks, are in the Bible. One of the greatest pieces of advice from my Pastor during our premarital counseling was to resolve arguments using the

Bible. In another words, refer to the blueprint for God's perspective on the particular issues in dispute.

The Bible states that we are his workmanship.[2] The Greek word for *workmanship* in that verse, is the word, "poeima," which literally means masterpiece. Just as Picasso, Stevie Wonder, and Rembrandt have delivered creative masterpieces, we are the very creative masterpieces of GOD. Now, we are not the only masterpieces that God created, but we are the apple of his eye! God is the supreme architect of man and woman and he has created us for specific purposes. Hence, nobody but God is more qualified to explain how man and woman should come together in the context of marriage. However, year after year, and marriage after marriage, the reality is that many husbands and many wives either never look at the blueprint or never refer back to it while or after laying the foundation. We try to change the building to suit our desires rather than adhering to the intended purpose and functionality of the building.

One of my favorite parts of the movie, "This Is It,"-- the documentary that follows Michael Jackson as he prepares for his last comeback tour, was when Jackson told the band that they were not playing the music correctly. They were making

---

[2] Ephesians 2: 10 (English Standard Version)

it funkier and putting sounds where they did not belong. An irritated Michael Jackson carefully demanded them to play it like he wrote it. Michael was not satisfied until they played the music precisely as he wrote it. Similarly, God will not be satisfied until we build the institution of marriage precisely as he designed it in the blueprint. Neither will spouses be satisfied either because true satisfaction and fulfillment can only come when we function in the ways God has ordained. This failure to follow the blueprint creates conflict because we live in a world where most people are dominated by self-gratification where we ask, "What have you done for me lately? What do I get out of this? How do I benefit?" Yet, when we truly understand the purpose of marriage, it will be easier to adhere to the tenets of it.

The major purpose of marriage is to **bring glory to God**. Please don't be offended by this truth. Just as a master musician who desires to make wonderful music may enlist several instruments and musicians to help bring the goal into a reality, God uses his children as accompanists. The composition starts in the mind of the master musician and the purpose is to make music that brings the master musician pleasure. What a privilege and an honor to be selected to play an instrument to assist the master musician. I could be upset and say "I want to create my own music." That is how Lucifer felt. Or, I can take joy in bringing the master musician pleasure. As creatures in his creation and instruments in his divine orchestra, we are playing so that God can get the standing ovation, not us. The fact that marriage is designed for God's glory should not be offensive because everything God designs is for his glory. While his glory is the primary purpose of marriage, there are four secondary **purposes** for marriage.

Marriage as a Picture:

The Bible is a story about the eternal marriage of Jesus Christ and his bride, the Church. The Old Testament depicts the marriage between God and his bride, Israel, which is a foreshadowing of the marriage between Christ and his church. The Bible chronicles the choosing of the bride, the courting, the paying of the dowry, the proposal, the preparing a place by the groom, the wedding, the giving away of the bride by the Father, and a glimpse of eternal fellowship. Much of our earthly ministry as Christians is to reflect the picture and process of God's perfect love. Marriage, therefore, is designed to show the world how God loves his people. When people see how two different and imperfect individuals are joined in marriage and become one, they can witness the power and love of God. In the book of Hosea, God commands his prophet Hosea to marry a prostitute. Really? Yes! This prophetic book chronicles how the husband, Hosea, time after time, goes after his wayward wife to bring her back home to him. This was a living portrait of how God loved his bride, Israel. When the world sees a love like that personified in a marriage, it illuminates the person and character of God.

Marriage for Procreation:

Marriage is the only holy context for sexual relations. More than the process of reproduction, God is interested in the fruit of the reproduction. Specifically, God tells Adam to be fruitful and multiply, fill, and subdue the earth. God ultimately wants an earth that is filled with righteous families who, generation after generation, give God glory. God also foreknew that he needed to send his Son in human flesh to redeem sinners. Even in the garden, God prophetically communicated that the seed of the woman would bruise the head of the serpent. For this prophecy to be fulfilled, there had to be procreation. Indeed, all of the great human contributors to God's holy plan arrived by procreation. Even if a married couple does not have or adopt children of their own, they can still be fruitful in how they sow into the lives of others around them.

Marriage for Partnership:

The marriage relationship was designed by God with the principle of partnership in mind. God created Eve and called her a "help meet" or "suitable helper." God gives Adam a strong, complimentary, and gifted partner to fulfill God's mandate to be "fruitful and multiply" and to "subdue the earth." Eve is not an inferior or lessor being; it is that Adam is inadequate to fulfill God's purposes and plan without her. Partnership at its best should result in agreement and unity. We see this picture in the Trinity. The concept of the Trinity, when referring to God, describes How God consists of three persons: Father, Son, and Holy Spirit, all perfectly unified as one. The members of the Trinity have different roles and responsibilities, yet are perfectly unified in all things. When husband and wife agree and are unified, God's blessings can be released in a major way.

Marriage for Perfection:

God uses the marriage laboratory to sanctify and mature us. God uses the most painful and irritating triggers from our past and places them in our spouses. As our fears, doubts, and "pet peeves" are triggered, they become instruments of healing. This is because they make it almost impossible not to depend on God. As we progressively yield and depend on

God, he heals and matures us through his Holy Spirit. A good way to understand this principle is in the example of the washing machine. The spinning contraption in the center of the machine is called an "agitator." The agitator, during several cycles, rubs hard against the clothing. This frequent or permanent press function is designed to put enough pressure on the fiber of the clothes to extract the dirt or stain so that the clothes are cleaned. Likewise, that is a main purpose of the marital relationship. God causes the issues of your spouse or your unresolved issues triggered by your spouse to permanently press upon you, in order to extract the stains from your character. The cleansing detergent is the Word of God found in the Bible, and the result of applying it is sanctification or maturity.

Distinct from the Godly purposes set forth above, many people get married because they have bought into the "fairy tale" that God designed marriage to make both the husband and wife happy. While joy, pleasure, and happiness are potential tertiary benefits of marriage, they are not the purpose for why God designed marriage. So before you say, "I do," make sure you carefully consult the blueprint. If you have already said, "I do," then circle back to the blueprint to ensure your marriage is functioning in the manner it was designed to function.

In case you are wondering whether God also designed marriage for our pleasure, he primarily designed marriage for *his* pleasure, not ours. However, an indirect benefit of marriage (next to honoring God) is to relate in covenant love with one's spouse. I have received so much pleasure knowing that God has gifted me with a wife that he hand-picked for me. Furthermore, when we follow the blueprint in our marriage, and experience all that God has ordained for us, the pleasure in indescribable. God wants spouses to enjoy intimacy, sexual fulfillment, companionship, affection, partnership, and many other blessings. Chapter 6 covers more about this.

Biblical Passages for Reflection:

Genesis 2:18-24

Jeremiah 29:1-11

Hosea 2:16-20

Ephesians 2:8-10

1 Peter 3:1-7

Summary Principles:

1) God is the architect of marriage.
2) The Bible is the blueprint of marriage.
3) Proper fidelity to the blueprint (which reflects the will and vision of the architect) ensures a successful marriage.
4) The major purpose of marriage is to bring God glory (not to bring us happiness).

The ***secondary purposes*** of marriage are:

Picture

Partnership

Procreation

Perfection

Simplified & Sanctified Exhortation (SSE):

Refer to God's Word (Holy Bible) as the blueprint during the preparation and process of marriage.

Prayer:

Father, let me rely on you and your Word to guide me in every major decision before and during my marriage in Jesus's name, Amen.

Journal

In what decisions have you consulted the Bible and in what decisions haven't you?

Chapter 2

Counting the Cost of Commitment

For which of you, desiring to build a tower, does not first sit down and count the cost, whether he has enough to complete it? (Luke 14:28)[3]

GLEAMING WITH THE joy and hope of a happy life together, Terry and Nicole came to my office to begin pre-marital counseling. This couple kept smiling at each other, and was giddy about the direction of their relationship. The courtship was short, but they were adamant that God had

[3] English Standard Version

joined them together. During the hour-long session, joy and excitement seemed to be the only emotion demonstrated until…until I mentioned money. I instructed the potential groom that it was his job to assume primary responsibility for financially providing for his wife and the household. Terry did not blink for he fully agreed with that statement. He had no problem with the notion of managing the $125,000.00 salary that his future wife earned. Now, please do not assume that Terry was not a hard worker. In fact, Terry is an extremely hard worker and earned around between $80,000.00 to $90,000.00 annually, depending on how much overtime he worked. He envisioned joining the two salaries, which would make them financially secure. Everything was pleasant during the session. until I made the statement that Terry did not want to hear. I said, "Terry, you need to prepare to live off of one salary. And, by one salary, I mean yours." The glee immediately turned to gloom. The confidence immediately turned to confusion. I explained to Terry that properly taking care of your wife means providing financially for her. In the session he said he understood, but I knew deep down he did not.

When we consider commitment in marriage, the cost can be categorized into two categories: *Building Costs* and *Maintenance Costs.* Under building costs, we will consider the following:

- The Cost of Marriage
- Due Diligence in Choosing a Mate
- Purity
- Premarital Counseling

Under maintenance costs, we will consider the following:

- Faithful Stewardship
- Blood
- Sweat
- Tears

Building Costs

The Cost of Marriage

Many department stores use what is called "price checkers." It is a mechanism that allows the customer to scan the item he/she is considering purchasing to see its cost. It is a great tool because if the price of the item is more than the customer can afford, he/she can return the item to the shelf. God's idea of marriage is very similar. Wisdom dictates that we count the cost of marriage before purchase. That's right, purchase! Before you buy the ring, pay the deposit for the wedding venue, and buy the bill of goods that the world has to offer, find out the cost. Invariably, couples dive into marriage without having a clear idea about what the true cost is. It is like commercials that advertise some great product as free. What you do not see is the small fine print which tells how much it will really cost.

Ecclesiastes 5:5 poignantly warns that it is better to not make a vow than to make a vow and not pay the vow.[4] Many people jump into marriage ill-prepared. They do not read the fine print on the advertisement. Hence, when the costs progressively accumulate, the refrain is "I did not know it was going to cost this much. I did not sign up for this!" When I conduct pre-marital counseling, I am very intentional about disclosing all of the foreseeable costs and even preparing the couple for the unforeseen costs. I would rather they make an informed decision than a blissful decision. In fact, I would

---

[4] English Standard Version

contend that the greatest decision-maker regarding marriage is often emotions. Whether the emotions are generated by sexual relations, infatuation, or "Hollywood fairytale optimism," the persons choosing to marry are usually oblivious to the hardline facts of how difficult a healthy marriage is.

In Luke's gospel, Jesus poses a very important question, "For which of you, desiring to build a tower, does not first sit down and count the cost, whether he has enough to complete it?"[5] This question that Jesus poses is found within a larger teaching on discipleship. Prior to that question, Jesus makes this piercing statement, "If anyone comes to me and does not hate his father and mother, wife, and children, brothers, and sisters, yes, and his own life also, he cannot be my disciple."[6] Ouch! Jesus, that is harsh! This does not sound like a message of love, Jesus! Proper interpretation of this passage, however, teaches us that Jesus is not promoting hatred. He is using the literary technique of hyperbole to exaggerate the cost of discipleship. He is saying that if you commit fully to follow Christ, it will require a radical reprioritizing of commitments. In other words, Jesus's agenda must trump everyone else's. Please notice that Jesus included wife and self in the category

---

[5] Luke 14:28 (English Standard Version)
[6] Luke 14:26 (English Standard Version)

of who must be "hated." Nobody, not even self or spouse, should be a higher priority than Jesus and his purposes. When Jesus explained this cost to a rich young ruler, the ruler went away sorrowfully as he was unwilling to pay the cost.

This instruction to count the cost of holy matrimony is not to instill fear, but to encourage preparedness. Even as I write this chapter, our local meteorologist just forecasted that a hurricane is approaching our region. The storm is a little too close for comfort. The warning or prognostication, however, allows me time to prepare to weather the storm. Likewise, I am forecasting that storms will undoubtedly come into your marriage. Some storms will register as category 3 hurricanes. If you prepare ***before*** you say, "I do," you can be ready and not surprised when the heavy winds begin to blow

One of the best ways to prepare for marriage is to utilize due diligence in the choosing of your potential spouse.

Due Diligence in Choosing a Mate

Michelle will turn 37 years old next week. Her excitement about having a birthday is competing with the anxiety and emotional rollercoaster ride she is experiencing because she is still single and childless. The time on Michelle's biological clock seems to be running out, and she has yet to find *Mr. Right*. She has dated *Mr. Sexy*, has lived with *Mr. Rich*, and was engaged to *Mr. Nice,* but none of the above relationships worked out. She tried the local bar scene, went on a few blind dates, and she even joined the singles ministry at church. Michelle now believes that her only hope is to use online dating to find her husband. She has constructed a "husband list" which details the qualities of her ideal husband. The top seven traits on Michelle's list include: (1) handsome (2) tall (3) rich (4) nice (5) no kids (6) athletic, and (7) sense of humor. Now, you may be thinking, "This is a good list" or "this resembles my list." Indeed, the characteristics that Michelle desires in her husband are not bad; however, they are not ***foundational***, and the foundation is the most important part of a building. If a building sits on the proper foundation, the building is expected to last even through destructive storms. Accordingly, Michelle's top characteristics for her husband should be traits that form a strong foundation for marriage.

Commitment over Compatibility

Online dating sites earn approximately one billion dollars per year as they advertise their main product--compatibility. They offer the ability to match profiles or allow their members to match profiles to find the most compatible match. The truth of the matter is that compatibility (as the world defines it) is not an important predictor of healthy marriage, but character is. Compatibility, in the context of human relationships, is the process where two people evaluate whether they can get along based on their likes, dislikes, philosophical worldview, their attractiveness, and other features. In the process of online dating, the more similarities between the two profiles, the greater the likelihood they will be matched. God's process is radically different. He does not match on similarity; rather he matches on divine purpose. The main reason why God created Eve for Adam was not because of emotional loneliness. God did not say to himself, "Adam looks pitiful! I need to make him a woman who is beautiful and sexy to cook for him and make him happy." No, Adam needed a "suitable helper" to fulfill the mandate of "being fruitful, multiplying, filling, and subduing the earth." Adam needed help in fulfilling his purpose.

The foundation of any building is inextricably tied to its purpose. The purpose of something is simply *why* it exists. Embedded in the *why* are the specific dimensions needed to build. The building is designed to fulfill some need or desire; consequently, the greater the need and/or desire the greater the undertaking. If the builder wants the building to be stable and secure for a long period of time, then he/she will make absolutely sure the building is laid on a proper foundation.

The successful endurance of marriage depends on the adherence to one's commitment. Therefore, choose a mate that consistently demonstrates in his/her character the proclivity to keep commitments even during difficult seasons. Many seeking marriage choose mates who have potential. In other words, they minimize the obvious flaws and focus on how they can change that person over time. Big mistake! Everyone has potential! Potential is like a seed. Every seed has the potential to become fruitful. However, every seed will not sprout. Many factors affect whether or not it does. The reality is that you have to wait and see after sowing. Every mate has potential. You need more than potential when choosing your mate. You need to see fruit on that potential mate's tree. The tree will not be fully ripened, but at least he/she is a lot closer to maturation. Marriage is designed to be permanent. Hence, one of the main characteristics one should look for in a spouse is the character trait to keep his/her commitments. Qualities like health, wealth, and beauty are transient like sand; however, one's true character generally remains the same over time.

I firmly believe that it is unwise and foolish to choose one's mate without seeking the wisdom of God. In my case, when I was ready to marry, I prayed that God would reveal to me the spouse he had ordained for me. Thank God I listened to his answer! However long it takes to be absolutely certain that the spouse you choose is God-approved is worth it. Do not rush into marriage without being convinced that he/she is the right one.

We will turn our attention to the wisdom of purity during the courting or engaged period.

Purity

Some people believe that it is impossible to remain a virgin until married in this present day and time. Or, many people consider it impossible to remain abstinent during the courting and engagement period. First, with God all things are possible! We can do all things through Christ who gives us strength. Second, I have witnessed couples adhere to the purity standards (no sex before marriage). So, it not only is possible, it happens. Not only does it happen, it is beautiful. The best reason why it is beautiful is because it is the mandate of God. As stated earlier, the marriage (not the courting, dating, or engaged) relationship is the *only* context where sexual relations are appropriate and acceptable to God.

Now, while it is possible, it does not mean that it is easy. The Apostle Paul writing to a church steeped in the sexual immoral culture of its time and location, Corinth, encouraged believers to marry rather than burn with passion.[7] That encouragement speaks to how difficult it is to remain single and sexually abstinent in a highly sexualized culture. Hence, below I provide practical recommendations to facilitate purity:

1) Court in public. Only enter into homes or locales together where other people are present to minimize temptation. Also, avoid "going away together."

2) Limit affection to short hugs and kisses. (not passionate)

3) Keep the engagement period short.

4) Watch and listen to Biblical, non-sexual material.

5) ***Pray Without Ceasing!***

We will now look at the benefits of premarital counseling.

---

[7] 1 Corinthians 7:9

Premarital Counseling

One of the biggest mistakes couples make is to marry without completing intensive premarital counseling. To fly a plane, one must submit to countless hours of instruction, studying, testing, and practice, before ultimately receiving a license. To become a physician, one must spend a minimum of eight years after high school attending classes and residencies, and one must pass the board exam to practice medicine. This intensive study is needed because pilot and doctor negligence can cause tremendous harm. Likewise, marital negligence can cause tremendous harm for generations. I know this because in my private practice, I see the vestiges of the dysfunction. The difference between being a spouse and being a pilot or a doctor is, that as a spouse, you are not legally required to adequately prepare to be a practitioner. All you need are two people who are willing to go to a courthouse or a church, or a celebrity (in certain states) to get married.

If you are married or were married and you did not have adequate premarital counseling, this discussion is not designed to upset you. Rather, it is designed to encourage you to know it is not too late. If you are engaged, seek intensive premarital counseling from an anointed and wise counselor;

and, if you are already married, but did not have adequate premarital counseling, you can still strengthen or repair an unstable foundation. I recommend submitting to marital counseling to specifically revisit the foundations that should have been laid before marriage.

I use the word "intensive" to mean that it should be thorough in terms of breadth and depth. It should be invasive as it is designed to pull some of what is hidden to the surface for analysis. So, if and when an engaged individual makes a commitment to marry, it is made knowing some major things about their potential spouse. Everything will not come out during premarital counseling, but with the right counselor and the right process, much should be revealed.

Some of the uncomfortable topics that should be excavated and addressed are sexual past (including homosexuality, molestations, pornography, prostitution, abortions, and diseases); current and past addictions (drugs, alcohol, gambling, work, etc.); past and current financial & debt status; and spiritual beliefs. Now, many people are afraid that their potential spouse will not marry them if they are open and honest about their past and current experiences. Here is my answer to that. If God has revealed that your fiancé is the "right one" and you intend to love her or him with the purest motivation of glorifying God, then the past should not matter if it really is in the past. That is the beautiful thing about *agape* love. *Agape* love is the godly, self-sacrificing love that always benefits others at the giver's expense. This is the love that the Apostle Paul describes in 1 Corinthians 13. Love covers a multitude of sins. More about this love will be discussed in chapter 6. Furthermore, how messed up was our past before Jesus married us? He knew exactly what he was getting into when he said, "I do and I will." Why start on a foundation of lies and deceit when you can start on the foundation of truth and honesty? Also, if your spouse falls in love with your image, what will happen when the images fades and the true picture comes to light? Finally, if your potential spouse cannot accept your true past and present self, is it not better to find that out ***before*** getting married?

Some pastors will not marry couples unless they go through sufficient premarital counseling. I support that notion. Due to God's grace, the intensive counseling and teaching that my wife and I completed before marriage, we have endured and continue to endure the storms that have arisen in our marriage.

We will turn our attention to the maintenance costs.

Maintenance Costs

Faithful Stewardship

Player, Ladies Man, and Playboy are words that once described Jonathan. He was never satisfied in a monogamous relationship; rather, like a successful hunter, he would rise up early and begin plotting how to conquer his prey. One day, Jonathan met a woman that seemed to change his outlook on chasing women. The woman, Diane, seemed to have everything Jonathan wanted and needed. Of course on the top of the list, she was physically beautiful. She had a pretty face and curves in all of the right places. Jonathan was smitten after just one glance. Diane was not only physically attractive, but she was confident, considerate, and graceful. Based on what Jonathan saw in and outside of Diane, he made a declaration that he would become a one-woman man. Jonathan was sincere in his *declaration* but naïve in his *preparation.* Diane knew he was a playboy, but thought she could change him. They began to date and for the first two weeks, Jonathan did not so much as look at another woman. However, one day Jonathan realized that Diane was not perfect. He noticed a flaw in her. Immediately, his devotion toward her slowly began to dissipate. Eventually, he found himself sleeping with another woman. Jonathan wanted to change, but his desire did not have the depth, the devotion, nor the discipline needed for true change.

Now, after reading about Jonathan, you may have become discouraged. However, not all men or women are like Jonathan. One of the greatest misconceptions in marriage is that it is, impossible and/or improbable that a man, in particular or any spouse, in general, can indeed be faithful. When we think of the word faithful with respect to marriage, we automatically think of not having sexual relations with another person other than one's spouse. As we explore the Biblical description of being faithful, we discover the Greek word in the New Testament, "pistos," which is most often translated faithful. It literally means *trustworthy.* It is derived from the root word "peitho" which means to convince. Hence, faithful, according to the Bible, means being dependable and trustworthy with convincing evidence.

It is an awesome responsibility to be married. This is because ultimately, we are stewards unto God and must give an account of our stewardship back to God. The Apostle Paul in his letter to the church at Corinth states that it is a requirement for stewards be found trustworthy.[8] This is a heavy statement! He is not suggesting that being faithful or

---

[8] 1 Corinthians 4:2 (English Standard Version)

trustworthy is *recommended* for stewards. He is saying that faithfulness or being trustworthy is a *requirement* for stewards. A steward is someone who has been entrusted with something or someone by the owner, and must give an account of how well he/she has protected, managed, invested, or improved upon the object of the trust. Marriage is an institution of stewardship. The husband has stewardship responsibility regarding his wife; and likewise, the wife has stewardship responsibility regarding her husband. Even though as stewards, spouses have responsibilities to each other, the primary obligation is to serve the owner. The primary reason why I love and take care of my wife is to demonstrate honor to God. I am going to have to give an account to him on how I handled this relationship. I want him to say, "Well done!"

Proper stewardship requires faithfulness, even through the years of BLOOD, SWEAT, and TEARS.

Blood

The payment of blood is twofold: First, it is the payment Jesus Christ made on our behalf in order to redeem us. Jesus Christ is the way, and the truth, and the life.[9] Without the

---

[9] John 14:6

blood of Jesus covering and cleansing us, the matrimony will never truly be holy. Once redeemed, however, the Holy Spirit lives within us to guide, teach, and lead us into all truth.[10] The good news regarding the blood is that we can benefit from Jesus's purposefully spilling his blood for us. The difficult news, involving the second payment of blood, is that we have some blood spilling of our own to do. Blood represents the life force of a human or animal. When you shed blood, you are losing life in a sense. Healthy marriage involves the dying to self, daily. This is very difficult. Who in their right mind would return to a relationship after being stabbed in the back by one's spouse? Metaphorical blood is still dripping and you return over and over again. That sounds foolish and sadomasochistic. Well, Jesus volunteered for the betrayal. He volunteered for the beatings and maligning of his character. He volunteered for death. Why? Simply stated; that was the cost of his loving commitment to his bride.

Husbands and wives are to die to self on a regular and consistent basis. We are to die to pride and to self-gratification. We are to die to self-seeking behavior and resist until we bleed. The writer of Hebrews encourages us by saying, "Consider him who endured from sinners such

---

[10] John 16:13

hostility against himself, so that you may not grow weary or fainthearted. In your struggle against sin you have not yet resisted to the point of shedding your blood."[11] The writer is likely comparing the process of resisting sin to the pugilistic boxing at the Grecian games. Those that participated in the boxing matches were usually covered in blood. The general sense of the passage is that while we have to shed blood in our wrestling (fighting), we do not have to pay the price paid by Christ and the apostles who were martyred. Our wrestling is the willful surrender of our selfish ways.

Sweat

Sweat represents hard work or effort. I tell my clients that having a healthy marriage is the hardest thing you may do in life. It is easy to have an unhealthy marriage. However, you must expend a tremendous amount of effort to invest in a healthy marriage. Marriage involves preparing the soil, sowing, watering and fertilizing, waiting, and then reaping. Using the gardening or farming paradigm, the ground work is the most labor intensive of the aforementioned processes. It involves digging, cultivating the soil, and removing rocks and weeds. The processes of watering and fertilizing and waiting, and reaping require less effort than the initial cultivating and

---

[11]Hebrews 12:3-4 (English Standard Version)

preparation work. Hence, the hardest part of the marital process occurs in the beginning. The first ten years of marriage are usually the hardest. They are the most labor intensive years. Much of the effort is removing the scores of baggage that both husband and wife brought into the marriage. This will be discussed further in Chapter 4.

Part of the reason why the marriage relationship will require tremendous effort is because of baggage called the fall of Adam and Eve. In Genesis 3, God handed out curses to both Adam and Eve. To Adam he said, "By the sweat of your face you shall eat bread, till your return to the ground."[12] Before the fall, Adam did not have to toil or utilize effort for food. To Eve, God said, "I will surely multiply your pain in childbearing; in pain you shall bring forth children. Your desire shall be for your husband, and he shall rule over you."[13] Therefore, the consequence of sin has added tremendous toil even in the marriage relationship.

Tears

Tears represent the intense pain that will permeate the marital relationship. Pain is not a visitor to the relationship; rather, pain lives with us and refuses to permanently leave.

---

[12] Genesis 3:19 (English Standard Version)
[13] Genesis 3:16 (English Standard Version)

The fairy tale about marriage where the couple lives happily ever after grossly distorts the reality. Mature marriages have joy in the midst of major tearful seasons. Joy is not the avoidance of pain. It is the disposition of faith and hope in God to bring the spouses through the difficult seasons. Consequently, when the season is over, the couple grows better, stronger, and wiser. Now, there will also be tears of joy. I have shed many tears of joy and gratitude over the course of my marriage. However, I have caused and received tremendous pain resulting in tears of pain and grief also.

In sum, as I mentioned earlier, this chapter is not meant to discourage you from getting married. Marriage is a wonderful and honorable institution. Just be sure to count the cost of the commitment. Before Jesus left the portals of glory, he knew the cost of marrying his bride — the church. He knew it would cost him suffering, grief, rejection, and death. Jesus counted the cost and, ultimately, paid the price, resulting in tremendous joy for our Lord. Hallelujah! Now, it is our turn!

Biblical Passages for Reflection

Luke 14:25-33

Proverbs 3:1-7

Ecclesiastes 5:1-6

Summary Principles:

1) Marriage is costly! Therefore, count the full (financial, emotional, physical, and spiritual) cost before you say, "I do."

2) Spouses are stewards. We must give an account to the owner (God).

3) It is wise to submit to *intensive* premarital counseling before marriage.

4) We are not wise enough to pick our spouses. Pray that God would reveal his choice for you. Study the character of your potential spouse's commitment level.

5) Remain pure (no sex) before marriage. It is possible with God, and it is required.

The ***major costs*** of marriage can be described as:

Blood

Sweat

Tears

Simplified & Sanctified Exhortation (SSE):

Only commit to marriage after you have counted and weighed the costs of marriage.

Prayer:

Father, let me make my commitment to marriage based on the true costs revealed in your Word and not a "fairy tale" myth, in Jesus's name, Amen.

Journal

After reading this chapter, are you really prepared for marriage? If already married, what do you need to change? Is the cost more than you expected?

THE PROCESS PHASE

PART II

Chapter 3

Marriage Simplified

The end of the matter; all has been heard. Fear God and keep his commandments, for this is the whole duty of man. For God will bring every deed into judgment, with every secret thing, whether good or evil. (Ecclesiastes 12:13-14)[14]

IF ANYONE KNOWS a thing or two about wisdom and relationships, it is King Solomon, arguably one of the wisest persons that has ever lived. The Bible records how God came to Solomon in a dream and invited him to ask anything of the

---

[14] English Standard Version

Lord. Solomon, who was newly appointed King of Israel, asked God for wisdom to properly lead God's people. God was so pleased with Solomon's request, that he gave Solomon great wisdom and great wealth, along with fame. In terms of relationships, Solomon had 700 wives and 300 concubines. That's a lot of women! Though he acted unwisely by letting his lust for women compromise his integrity in worshipping God alone, his experiential failures and successes have produced a major pearl of wisdom that will help us. In fact, this pearl of wisdom is the very thesis of this book. It is found in the book of Ecclesiastes. He ends the book of Ecclesiastes with these thoughts, "The end of the matter; all has been heard. Fear God and keep his commandments, for this is the whole duty of man. For God will bring every deed into judgment, with every secret thing, whether good or evil."[15] Wow! The wise preacher's thesis statement on life is to *fear God and keep his commandments*. Similarly, the simple secret for having a sanctified marriage is to ***fear God and to keep his commandments***. Fear means to respect his position of sovereign authority, and keep his commandments means to obey him. In other words, have such a tremendous respect for

[15] Ecclesiastes 12:13-14 (English Standard Version)

the architect of marriage that you purpose to follow the blueprint as closely as possible.

During my academic years, math was not my strongest subject. I was not mathematically illiterate, but let's just say that math was the only subject for which I ever needed a tutor. I had to repeat algebra 1 and trigonometry was hilarious to me. When given a test, I perfected new ways of guessing the right answer on the multiple choice portions. Passing calculus in college definitely required divine intervention. However, there was one concept in mathematics in which I excelled. I was good at simplifying fractions. I could, quite easily, reduce fractions with huge numerators and denominators to their simplest form. Similarly, this chapter reveals how to take the complexity of marriage and simplify it.

I was taught in school that to simplify fractions, one had to divide the numerator and the denominator by the greatest common factor. For example, when 18/27 is divided by 9/9, the simplified answer is 2/3. We can understand two out of three better than 18 out of 27. The simplification process does not change the essence of the numbers, rather, it gives us a mechanism and methodology to understand the numbers better. This book on marriage is not based on new or radically different information. It is simply presented in a way to understand what a sanctified marriage looks like in a simplified manner.

The Dividends of Marriage

Holy matrimony is indeed a very complex institution, and often we get lost in its minutia. The deeper we delve into the minutia, the blinder we are to the big picture. The big picture of a sanctified marriage is three-fold. Marriage is about *glory*, *maturity*, and *influence*. God gets the glory, and we have the blessed privilege to influence others, while God is progressively maturing us. In a word, marriage is about ***dividends***. Dividends are represented in the glory God receives from your marriage, and the tangible impact your marriage can have on someone else.

In investing, dividends are payments that corporations give to their shareholders, a benefit given as the corporation increases in profitability. The corporation benefits first and then the shareholder benefits. That is how it is with God's holy corporation called marriage. When the shareholders (married couples) invest in marriage, three things happen. First, God, the founder of marriage, benefits by receiving glory. Now, we do not add to God's glory; rather, we reflect and refract his glory which brings him honor and pleasure.

Second, the investors receive dividends in the form of blessings. The blessings received not only bless the receivers, but are also magnets that attract others to marvel and quench their curiosity. In between the glory and influence is the maturation process which benefits the investors directly. The maturation process does not always feel like a benefit, but it is beneficial. I know this notion might not sit right with many people. Many people have been socialized to believe that the primary purpose of marriage was so they could be happy and experience consistent pleasure. Hollywood perpetuates this misconception. However, it is not Hollywood's job to develop mature marriages; that is the job of the Church of Jesus Christ. When we radically reclaim our responsibilities in holy matrimony, we then can bring God more glory and have more influence in our marriages.

The simple exhortation of this book is that ***we, spouses, need to love God by loving our spouses.*** This is the simplest formula for holy matrimony. Notice that I did not say love God **and** love spouse. Notice that I did not say love God **or** love spouse. I said love God ***by*** loving your spouse. If the highest reach of our motive is to please our spouse or even to please ourselves, we will undoubtedly arrive at a point where we deem the process to be "not worth it." The marriage fairy tale is based on the lie that pleasure and happiness will sustain the couple throughout the marriage. It is akin to binging on sugar or any other addictive drug. The high is great and pleasurable. The difficulty arises when the high wears off and you have to deal with the lows. One of the reasons the Apostle Paul wished that the Corinthians, in particular, and people, in general, did not get married was so that their devotion to God would not be compromised with the anxieties of life. Paul specifically states, "Yet those who marry will have worldly troubles, and I would spare you that."[16] Paul further states,

> *I want you to be free from anxieties. The unmarried man is anxious about the things of the Lord, how to please the Lord. But the married man is anxious about worldly things, how to please his wife, and his interests are divided. And the unmarried or betrothed woman is anxious about the things of the Lord, how to be holy in body and spirit. But the married woman is anxious about worldly things, how to please her husband.* [17]

The Apostle Paul is being quite honest with the challenge of being married while still making God the number one priority. For many, it definitely appears to be more difficult to prioritize God when tasked with loving a spouse. However, the concept of loving God by loving your neighbor is a common theme in scripture. The Apostle John says in 1 John

---

[16] 1 Corinthians 7:28 (English Standard Version)
[17] 1 Corinthians 7:32-34 (English Standard Version)

4:20, "If anyone says, I love God, and hates his brother, he is a liar; for he who does not love his brother whom he has seen cannot love God whom he has not seen."[18] The major principle of that verse, this chapter, and this book is that ***the way we love one another, especially our spouse, is a direct reflection of how we love God.*** The best demonstration of loving God is not singing in the choir, giving money in the offering, nor preaching or teaching; rather, it is loving one another. Indeed, the spousal relationship is a closer relationship than even one's neighbor. When we become Christians, we become the "body of Christ." When Christ loves his church — his bride, he is loving his own body. We are now one! Well, we ought to love our spouses like we love our bodies.

This is precisely the charge that Paul gives to the church at Ephesus (Ephesians 5:28-30),

> *In the same way husbands should love their wives as their own bodies He who loves his wife loves himself. For no one ever hated his own flesh, but nourishes and cherishes it, just as Christ does the church, because we are members of his body.*[19]

---

[18] English Standard Version
[19] English Standard Version

Since marriage means that husband and wife becomes one flesh, there is nobody closer to us except for God.

My argument is that the marital relationship is the best picture to see how much we really love God. We are tested daily and given the opportunity to show love and obey God on a consistent basis. The Apostle Paul in Galatians 6:10 exhorts that we should do good deeds especially to the "household of faith." We should love everybody; however, we should be careful to be especially loving to those who are a part of the same body of Christ. Of all the people in the world, our love for God should be most reflected in the marital relationship. The concept of loving God by loving spouse can be further described by the following principles: **worship**, **witness**, and **wisdom**.

Worship

Often, when many people think about worship, they think about a choir, a hymn book, and parishioners singing or dancing in church. Well, the first time we see the word "worship" in the Bible, it is mentioned in the context of Abraham preparing to sacrifice his beloved son, Isaac.[20] Abraham went up to Mount Moriah to offer Isaac as an

---

[20] Genesis 22:5

offering to God. There were no choirs, no organs, and no singing or dancing on the mountain. Abraham worshiped simply with *obedience.* Worship can be distilled into one word, obedience.

Every human being is born with the proclivity to worship. The question is who we worship. If we buy into the fairy tale that life and marriage is about my happiness, then we are most likely going to worship ourselves. Some people actually worship their spouses, relying on them as the only one to bring them happiness. They make statements like, "you are my world" or "you are my everything!" Those, however, are unhealthy statements if made about another human being. The truth about humans is that no matter the level of sincerity, humans frequently let other humans down.

Loving your spouse is and should be an act of worship. The spouse is not the ***object*** of worship, but presents an ***opportunity*** to worship God by honoring the covenant of marriage. ***This is so vital to understand***! Everything you do in the marriage should be an offering to God. Many spouses do things or refuse to do things based on emotions, or the performance of the other spouse, or other reasons. Whatever reason you choose to justify your unloving words and behavior toward your spouse is unacceptable, unjustifiable, and ultimately not God glorifying. I know this sounds harsh, however, we make excuses for why we treat our spouses in ways that disobey God.

Here is the awesome truth about worshiping God in marriage. ***If one's deepest desires and actions honor God, they will undoubtedly be in the best interest of one's spouse and marriage.*** This is because *everything* God does for us is in our best interest. So, when I honor God by loving my spouse, his name is glorified. Before I consider the earthly impact on my spouse, my family, or on myself, the first and most important priority is to glorify God. So when I choose to forgive, it is to honor God. When I decide to sacrifice or deny myself, it is first to glorify God. When I choose to work hard to care for my wife, it is an offering unto God. When I choose to not give up on the marriage in seasons of pain and seeming dysfunction, I do it to glorify him. When I decide to be faithful to my wife, I do it to glorify God first and foremost, then to love her second.

A sacrificial offering is thus defined because it costs you something. When I make up my mind to do the aforementioned things, I decide to do them not because I feel like doing them; rather, I do them because that is how much my offering costs. When Jesus made the decision to die on the cross, the primary motivation for enduring so much pain was to glorify the Father. Some people who may read this section may think that this is overly spiritual. You may even say, "I am not Jesus." Well, Christians are supposed to be like him. We are to talk like him, walk like him, suffer like him, and love like him. His spirit that lives within every Christian gives us the ability to act like him.

Now, let us discuss the impact of our witness.

Witness

Ultimately, God wants our marriages to be witnesses of the unfailing, steadfast, and loving relationship that God has with his people. A witness is someone who sees or experiences something and can therefore testify to its veracity. God wanted the nation of Israel to be a kingdom of priests. He wanted his people to be the example of what it means to have God provide for and protect you, and fulfill his promises. He wanted Israel to testify to other nations about God's goodness and dependability. When we get to heaven, the only marriage that will exist will be the marriage between Christ and his church. We will not need to continue the marriages that were established on earth because the need for the witness marriage provides will no longer exist.

When we look at marriage in an evangelistic light, healthy marriages are vehicles that can bring people to God's kingdom. God revealed to me early on in my marriage that my marriage was bigger than me and my wife. Now I understand! My wife and I witnessed to our five children about love, covenant, forgiveness, and obedience through our example. We also exposed them to church, Sunday School, reading the Bible, and Christian themed music, encouraging their hearts and minds to believe. I am grateful today that all five of my children have accepted Jesus as their Lord and Savior. If you have no children, then the people closest to you become your evangelistic mission field. My parents have been married for over 55 years. What a profound witness for me and my siblings as well as all that know them.

A silent witness can be powerful if his/her actions speak volumes; however, the best witnesses are those who witness both with their words and their deeds, especially after overcoming trials and difficulties. What describes a healthy marriage is not perfection, but overcoming seasons of mistakes, dysfunction, selfishness, and addiction, to realize a constant lifestyle of faith in God demonstrated by obedience. When spouses can testify with words and actions about how God has matured their marriage through difficult seasons, it points to God's greatness. Not only that, the witness gives other couples hope that their marriage can turn the corner. I have heard many persons speak about how they do not know married couples in their circle who have a healthy marriage. This is tragic! How is God glorified when the institution he founded seems to be more and more defunct? On the other hand, the witness from a healthy and transparent marriage can breathe life into these seemingly defunct marriages.

Next, let us look at the principle of wisdom in the marriage.

Wisdom

Proverbs 9:10 states, "The fear of the LORD is the beginning of wisdom, and the knowledge of the Holy One is insight."[21] This means that the ability to make wise decisions emanates from a respect of God and from the internalization of his revelations. In simple language, when couples obey God's instructions with a sincere motivation to honor him, they will be successful in marriage. I know it sounds overly simplistic, but that is the beauty of wisdom. God's wisdom is simple! We as humans struggle because we want to think for ourselves and make our own decisions. We often tell God with our words and our actions, "Thank you but no thank you.

[21] English Standard Version

I will make this decision for myself." This is when disaster happens.

Proverbs 11:30 states, "The fruit of the righteous is a tree of life, and whoever captures souls is wise."[22] Wisdom gives spouses the ability to literally give people life and capture souls for good. I tell my children, "You are Gradys!" What you say, what you do, and how you live reflects on the name Grady. Well, how we relate in our marriages reflects on the name of the Lord. When we speak wisdom and act wisely in our marriages, God is glorified. Wisdom is not some ancient, esoteric or ethereal body of information. Vine's Complete Expository Dictionary[23] defines wisdom is as technical skills or special abilities in fashioning something. Wisdom, in the context of marriage, is internalizing God's instructions on marriage and following them precisely, while developing specific abilities in order to fashion a marriage that glorifies God. In other words, it is adhering as closely as possible to the blueprint. A good example of this is when Apostle Peter got out of the boat and began to walk on water. He was able to perform this miracle because his eyes were fixed on God (Jesus). The moment he took his eyes off of Jesus and looked at his circumstance, he began to sink. How many times have

---

[22] English Standard Version

[23] Hebrew word for wisdom (hokmāh)

couples taken their eyes off of God, and focused them on the difficulties and dysfunction of their spouse and/or marriage? Wisdom dictates that the fear of the Lord anchors true decision-making. This is where couples must distinguish between pop culture and the wisdom of the Bible. Those who stand firmly on the wisdom of the Bible relating to marriage will be labeled radical, old-fashioned, and insensitive. However, the more those wise couples apply God's simplistic wisdom for life and marriage, the more successful and joyful life and their marriage will become. Many marriages fail or are headed down the trajectory of failure because they entertain the "wisdom" (foolishness) of popular culture.

I will end this chapter with Proverbs 14:12 which states, "There is a way that seems right to a man, but the end is the way to death."[24] Some decisions may seem and feel right, but if the decisions do not align with the blueprint, destruction is inevitable. Many couples have asked me to help them cope with their impending divorce. After showing them God's blueprint for marriage, many of them have reconciled! God's wisdom is always better!

---

[24] English Standard Version

Biblical Passages for Reflection

Ecclesiastes 12:13-14

Proverbs 14:12

Proverbs 9:10-11

Colossians 3:17

Ephesians 5:28-30

Summary Principles:

1) The simple secret to having a healthy marriage is to love your spouse as an act of worship to God.

2) If your deepest motive is to obey God in your marital decisions, you can be assured that those decisions will be in your spouse's and in your marriage's best interest.

3) Marriage is about glory, maturation, and influence. God gets the glory and I have the privilege of influencing others in my marriage, while being matured.

The principles which describe the simplicity of a holy and healthy marriage are:

1. **Worship**

2. **Witness**

3. **Wisdom**

Simplified and Sanctified Exhortation (SSE):

Love God by loving your spouse!

Prayer:

Father, please impress upon me this simplistic truth that how I love my spouse is an offering unto you. Empower me to remove the excuses and rationalizations away so I will not be hindered in obeying you. In Jesus's name, Amen.

Journal

Are you purposefully loving your spouse as an act of worship to God? How or Why Not?

Chapter 4

The Sanctified Marriage

Sanctify them in the truth; your word is truth[25]

MARRIAGE IS MORE about holiness than happiness. We often incorrectly conceptualize the marriage relationship as a lifetime of pleasure and happiness. Even though pleasure and happiness are secondary benefits, the primary purpose of marriage is the glory and honor due to God's name. God is in the business of holiness. God says in Leviticus 20:26, "You

[25] John 17:17 (English Standard Version)

shall be holy to me, for I the LORD am holy and have separated you from the peoples, that you should be mine."[26] In that verse, God was speaking to his bride, Israel, about his expectations of her. Specifically, God had chosen Israel from all of the nations on the earth to be holy and distinct from everyone else. God also expected that Israel would be faithful to her husband. Likewise, the same exhortation is given to Christians in the New Testament. Peter exhorts in 1 Peter 1:16, "Since it is written, you shall be holy, for I am holy."[27] As Christians, we are compelled by God to be holy. Holiness distinguishes Christians from all other peoples; and, when we live holy, we are honoring God.

One of the best ways God chooses to sanctify us or to make us holy is in the context of marriage. The marriage relationship is a microcosm of the local church. In the local church, there should be consistent worship, Bible instruction, exhortation, and fellowship designed to make the parishioners more like Christ. Furthermore, the instruction and inspiration we receive at church should empower us for ministry in the world. Similarly, the marriage has the same goal. God wants there to be worship, Bible instruction, exhortation, and fellowship which result in the sanctification of the whole

---

[26] English Standard Version
[27] English Standard Version

family, beginning with the marriage. Then, God wants the maturing couple to be a public example of the holiness and love of God.

One of the reasons why God chooses the marriage relationship as an incubator for sanctification is the potential for intimacy within the marital fellowship. Let me explain. "Fellowship" in the New Testament is the Greek word *koinonia*. It describes a communion or a gathering where all of the members of that community have all things in common. In many of the ancient Greek tragedies, the actors, called hypocrites, usually wore masks to hide their true identity. One of the practical reasons for the hypocrites wearing a mask was because the same actor had to play different roles. Many spouses are like the ancient "hypocrites" who are wearing masks while playing various different roles. It was only after the play ended when the actors would take their masks off. That fellowship was called "koinonia." The intimacy and interrelatedness could occur because their masks were removed. The true identity, which was hidden, was now gleaned through true fellowship. True fellowship could happen because the people were unmasking themselves.

Similarly, we all come into the theater of life with masks on. There is some insecurity, some deficiency, some shame, or some guilt that we are attempting to hide. As long as the mask is on, there is detachment. We often lose ourselves in the role or image we are portraying or projecting. The marriage relationship, however, makes wearing masks difficult. Your spouse, especially after years and years of togetherness, likely knows you better than any other person, including your parents. Furthermore, your spouse may know you better than you even know yourself. You may appear to be clean and well put together in public, but your spouse may know you to be a slob at home. You may appear to be religious and of high moral character in public, but your spouse is privy to your many indiscretions. Here is the point, sanctification happens sooner when our masks are taken off. It is easier for me to repent and change when I know my issues, God knows my issues, and my wife knows my issues. I do not need to hide anymore. I can take off my mask, be healed, and mature to become more holy.

This sanctification in marriage is three-dimensional. First spouses are sanctified ***from*** **their past**. Second, spouses are sanctified ***in*** **his presence**; and third, spouses are sanctified ***for*** **their divine purpose**.

Sanctified from Past

No matter how uneventful and vanilla we think our pasts were, we all bring significant baggage into the marriage relationship. Remember, every human being is born in sin and is shaped in iniquity. We are not born with a "tabula rasa" or blank slate; rather, we are born with a proclivity towards evil and selfishness. On top of that, family dysfunctional patterns shape our learning. While dysfunctionality is relative, we all bring loads of dysfunction into the marriage. If nothing else, we bring selfishness to the table. Many people who are married have very traumatic and negatively impactful pasts. God wants to use the marriage relationship as a sanctifying mechanism to purge us of our unhealthy and unholy pasts. Before God brings out the best in us, He has to reveal the worst in us.

Triggers

God, in his sovereign wisdom, purposefully uses one spouse to "trigger" the issues and insecurities of the other spouse. Thanks, God! (*Sarcasm*) Inevitably, one spouse has patterns, tendencies, and idiosyncrasies that trigger or remind the other spouse about a painful time in his/her past. Most of the time, the spouse who is doing the triggering does not know what he/she is doing. They are just being themselves.

However, God uses that dynamic to trigger and ultimately bring to the surface the issues that need to be addressed or resolved.

I often ask my clients to identify the most powerful part of a gun. Invariably, they will say the trigger. They believe this because pulling the trigger unleashes the power. The correct answer, however, is not the trigger, but the bullet. If you remove bullets from the gun, you can pull the trigger repeatedly and nothing will happen. Healing involves taking the bullets — the painful and dysfunctional past out of the gun. When the trigger is pulled in the relationship, the power of one's past trauma and dysfunction does not have to be unleashed. The problem, however, is that when pain and insecurities are triggered, spouses tend to blame the spouse who triggered the pain, rather than own up their own issues being revealed.

In the context of being sanctified, God is adamant about wanting to heal us and purge us of dysfunctionality in order to make us holy. When spouses understand this principle, they will more readily submit to the healing process occurring within themselves instead of blaming the one that keeps pulling the trigger.

Marital Agitation

I liken the process of marriage to the permanent press cycle on the washing machine, first referenced in chapter one. Old washing machines contained an internal device called an "agitator." The agitator applied permanent pressure during the cycle with the purpose of extracting the dirt and stains from the fiber of the clothing. That is what God does in marriage. He uses the agitating, triggering tendencies of our spouses to facilitate the extraction of stains in our character, specifically, the stains that were developed from the past. To put in plainly, God uses each spouse to agitate the other spouse for the purposes of sanctification or holiness. When I explain this process to couples, they can attest to its validity, but almost never was it explained to them prior to getting married. Yet, there is usually full agreement from both spouses, that the other spouse is anointed to agitate them.

Sanctified in His Presence

The Apostle Paul states in Ephesians 5:25-27:

> *Husbands, love your wives, as Christ loved the church and gave himself up for her, that he might sanctify her, having cleansed her by the washing of water with the word, so that he might present the church to himself in splendor, with spot or wrinkle, or any such*

thing, that she might be holy and without blemish.[28]

The goal of marital sanctification is to create holy spouses. This concept or description of holiness is not an outward religiosity; rather, an inward process where the fruits of the spirit (love, joy, peace, patience, kindness, goodness, faithfulness, gentleness, self-control) can be ripened. Please notice from the above scripture that the sanctification process is undergirded by love. Christ loved the church and gave himself for her that he might sanctify her. God sanctifies us because he loves us. Spouses should sanctify each other because of love. God loves us enough to not allow us to stay unholy. Just as a parent will discipline and correct a child to better the child, God does the same for us. He continually corrects us and disciplines his children so that we will look less like our past and more like Jesus. The principles that describe the sanctifying process in God's presence are **conviction**, **confession**, and **correction.**

Conviction

The cleansing agent in the sanctification process is the Holy Spirit. One of the primary works of the Holy Spirit is to convict us of wrongdoing while, simultaneously, leading us to

[28] English Standard Version

what is right. The Holy Spirit is our inner prosecutor who reveals to us that we have transgressed God's law. The Holy Spirit can communicate directly with our spirits but is most effective when working through Scripture. The best way God sanctifies spouses is through his Holy Bible. There are many spouses or couples preparing to get married and they are adamant about some of their decisions. Usually, if the decision is wrong, the future spouse offers a multi-layered rationalization which justifies the decision. I will typically then ask the client to identify the Biblical verse or passage that endorses said decision. Most individuals who use the Bible to justify their wrong decisions usually misquote it or take scripture passages out of context, leading to self-serving and subjective beliefs but no sanctification. Therefore, we need an authority figure higher than ourselves to tell us when we are wrong. That authority is God who has revealed himself through his holy Word. Even when the lawmakers in society legislate sinful practices, we are still governed and convicted by God and God's Word. In God's sanctifying process, when one is convicted, confession should follow.

Confession

Confessing to one's spouse should be secondary to our confession to God. God is always the offended party when we sin. Confession means talking to God about our sin. It means saying the same thing about our decision that God says in his Word. A lack of confession is where a major breakdown occurs in marriage. In a marital context when people hear the word confession, they think of confessing to their spouse. The breakdown occurs when we are convicted internally but refuse to confess. Many parents can attest to the following scenario: You catch your child in a lie or doing something wrong and he/she is caught red-handed. As the parent, you are waiting for the admission of guilt and perhaps an apology. Instead of confessing, however, often the child either sticks to his/her lie or attempts to justify that behavior. Unfortunately, this process makes it difficult to learn the lesson because the child has yet to confess that what he/she said or did was truly wrong. This is the pattern in so many marriages. We are wrong. We know we are wrong. Our spouses know we are wrong. God knows we are wrong. Our children know we are wrong. However, instead of confessing the wrongdoing and accepting the correction, we change the focus from ourselves to someone else -- usually our spouses. This cycle keeps many spouses stuck. Confession, on the other hand, is a great thing for the following reasons:

1. **Confession is a prerequisite to true healing**. James 5:16 states, "Therefore, confess your sins to one another and pray for one another, that you may be healed."[29]

2. **Confession leads to forgiveness and cleansing**. 1 John 1:9 states, "If we confess our sins, he is faithful and just to forgive us our sins and to cleanse us from all unrighteousness."[30]

3. **Confession removes the weight and burden of the secret or sin**. Hebrews 12:1 states, "Therefore, since we are surrounded by so great a cloud of witnesses, let us also lay aside every weight, and sin which clings so closely, and let us run with endurance the race that is set before us."[31]

Correction

Confession does not eliminate the need for correction. It, instead, positions the confessor with the right attitude and disposition to accept the correction. If I really want to be holy and give God the most glory possible, then I will submit to correction as I know correction will make me better. God's correction will make me more holy. God's correction is intended to help us **change**. If you really want to change your

---

[29] English Standard Version
[30] English Standard Version
[31] English Standard Version

behavior and character, let God correct you. The Bible states that God disciplines the one He loves.[32] Godly correction is a function of agape love. Agape love, as mentioned before, is the godly, self-less love which always benefits the one receiving the love. When spouses accept God's correction, radical change can and will occur. When God corrects us in the sanctification process, we are assured of His promise that He will never leave or forsake us.

One of the most popular yet misunderstood verses is Romans 8:28. It says,

> *And we know that for those who_love God*
> *all things work together for good, for those*
> *who are called according to his purpose.*[33]

Please understand, the verse does not say that all things **will be** good, it says that all things **work together** for good. This description "for good" is understood best in the context of the next verse, which states,

> *For those whom he did foreknew he also*
> *predestined to be conformed to the image of*
> *his Son, in order that he might be thee*
> *firstborn among many brethren.*[34]

[32] Hebrews 12:6a (English Standard Version)
[33] English Standard Version
[34] English Standard Version

In describing the sanctification process, Paul states that all things will work together for good in our conformation to the image of Christ. God will use whomever and whatever to make us like Jesus. He will use success and failure, sickness and health, and riches and poverty to accomplish his divine pottery. When God corrects, he is simply making us better. The sooner we submit to the correction, the sooner we become better.

Sanctified for our Purpose

We have discussed being sanctified from our past and being sanctified in his presence. Let us now discuss being sanctified for our purpose. In the context of ministry, sanctification means to be set apart for a holy purpose. Again, the primary purpose of a husband and wife is to bring God as much glory as possible through their marriage. There are ministry opportunities that God wants to extend to couples; however, sin renders the couple ineligible for that opportunity or assignment. We are often distracted by the mundane things of life that we miss out on ministry opportunities. What motivates me to submit to the correction of God and confess my mistakes is my desire to let God use my marriage and family for his purposes. I want us to have the influence that God has destined for us to have, and to, likewise, enjoy the many blessings of a sanctified marriage. As I look at our influence, inside and outside of the home, I continue to ask God to make us more and more holy. Our sanctification is not just about us, but it is about the people we are supposed to influence for good. I do not just bathe because I do not like the way I smell. I am mindful of how my scent can negatively impact the people around me. I do not want people to be turned away from my influence because I stink. Similarly, when the scent of our lifestyles is rotten and polluted, we are unable to positively affect the people God has entrusted to us. You may not know the specifics of your purpose yet. However, the road that takes us there begins with recognizing our unholy past, and as we spouses submit to the sanctifying work of God, God will lead us to that particular purpose.

Biblical Passages for Reflection

Romans 8:28-29

Hebrews 12:6a

Ephesians 5:25-27

James 5:13-19

1 John 1:5-10

Summary Principles:

1) We are sanctified ***from* our past**.
2) We are sanctified ***in* his presence**.
3) We are sanctified ***for* our purpose**.
4) While in his presence, we are sanctified through **conviction**, **confession**, and **correction**.

Simplified & Sanctified Exhortation:

Submit to the sanctifying process where God convicts and corrects us so we will be like Christ.

Prayer:

Father, give me the courage to confess my faults and ways to you, while submitting to your process of making me and my marriage more holy. I know that you will use every pain I experience to make me more holy and to have greater godly influence in others. Even when I am stubborn, please persist for I do want my marriage to be sanctified. In Jesus's name, Amen.

Journal

What tendencies have you yet to confess to God? Write the areas of your marriage where you refuse to submit to the authority of the Bible.

Chapter 5

AS

Therefore be imitators of God, as beloved children. And walk in love, as Christ loved us and gave himself up for us a fragrant offering and sacrifice to God[35]

ONE OF STEVIE Wonder's signature masterpieces from his "Songs in the Key of Life" album is a song entitled, "As."

Wonder poetically writes these lyrics:

[35] Ephesians 5:1-2

> *As around the sun the earth knows she's revolving and the rosebuds know to bloom in early may; just as hate knows love's the cure you can rest mind assure that I'll be loving you always; as now can't reveal the mystery of tomorrow but in passing grow older every day; just as all that's born is new you know what I say is true that I'll be loving you always*[36]

The writer uses the simile "as" to poetically describe how he will love the object of his love for always. In that stanza, Wonder compares the consistency and predictability of nature to his consistent and unfailing love for the object of his love. Though the song is very poetic and romantic, with the current climate of "love" and marriage lasting far shorter than always, many people longing for the type of love Wonder writes about may consider the song to be idealistic and unrealistic poetic fiction. The Bible, however, personifies love perfectly in the person of God. How God loves becomes a perfect paradigm for us to emulate. Though we will always fall short in our pursuit to love exactly as God loves, we at least have a perfect example by which to measure our progress.

In the New Testament of the Bible, another phenomenal writer uses "as" to emphasize how husbands and wives are to love each other. The apostle Paul exhorts, "Wives, submit to your own husbands, **as** to the Lord. For the husband is the

---

[36] Lyrics from the song, "As" (Stevie Wonder)

head of the wife even **as** Christ is the head of the church, his body and is himself its Savior. **As** the church submits to Christ, so also wives should submit in everything to their husbands."[37] Granted, I know that many women wish these verses were not in the Bible for a couple of reasons. First, many men misinterpret the passage and subsequently use the verses as a spiritual justification for their dictatorial domination. Another reason is that many women feel like the concept of submission limits their freedom. The true object of our submission, however, should be the Lord Jesus Christ. He, in fact, is the Lord and Savior to those who are born again and redeemed by his blood. Hence, Paul qualifies the command to submit by saying "as unto the Lord." This command does not mean that the wife decides whether the husband is submitting to Christ in a particular situation; and on that basis, she decides whether she is going to submit. If that were the case, the text would read, "Wives, when you believe your husband is submitting to Christ, obey him. Otherwise, trust yourself." When a Christian woman says, "I do," she is entering into a covenant marriage where the husband is her head. Submission has less to do with the

[37] Ephesians 5:22-24

spouse's performance; it has more to do with the spouse's position. This position is something God ordained.

In the same vein, husbands are mandated to submit directly to Christ. The process of loving and leading one's wife is patterned after Christ's love for and leadership of His church. First and foremost, husbands are also supposed to submit. They are to submit directly to Jesus Christ for Christ is the head of the man (husband). In submitting directly to Christ, he becomes an agent of his perfect love directed toward their spouses. It also behooves husbands to submit to the wisdom and giftedness that God gives to their wives. If my wife is truly my suitable helper, then she has ideas, experiences, wisdom, expertise, vision, and insight that is beneficial for both me and my family. I would be foolish (I sometimes have been) in not yielding to her wisdom when I know that deep down that particular wisdom is from God. In chapter 6 (Covenant Love), I will discuss in more detail the concept of *Hesed* which speaks of God's covenant love with his chosen bride, Israel. Husbands have a covenant responsibility to love their wives the same way Christ loves his bride.

After Paul writes the exhortation to wives to submit to their own husbands, he writes one to husbands as follows:

Husbands, love your wives, as Christ loved the church and gave himself up for her, that he might sanctify her, having cleansed her by the washing of water with the word, so that he might present the church to himself in splendor, without spot or wrinkle or any such thing, that she might be holy and without blemish... "In the same way husbands should love their wives as their own bodies. He who loves his wife loves himself." ... "For no one ever hated his own flesh, but nourishes and cherishes it, just as Christ does the church, because we are members of his body.

Paul ends chapter 5 by stating, "However, let each one of you love his wife as himself, and let the wife see that she respects her husband."[38]

Please note, the aforementioned verses in Ephesians 5 are not solely about submission. Submission is a principle idea, but it does not paint the full picture. The chief exhortation of Ephesians 5 is found in verses one and two. It reads,

Therefore be imitators of God, as beloved children. And walk in love, as Christ loved us and gave himself up for us, a fragrant offering and sacrifice to God.[39]

Once again, we see the word *as* present. The simple command and exhortation is to love one another as Christ loved and still loves us. A frequently used excuse I hear from couples is that they do not know how to love their spouses like Christ loved them. Yet, the pattern is clearly outlined in the

---

[38] English Standard Version
[39] English Standard Version

Bible. If you really want to follow the pattern, you can. Below, I discuss the principles that will help you follow the pattern of Christ in your marriage. They are **model**, **means**, and **motivation**.

Jesus is always our frame of reference or **model**, even in marriage. Hence, we should be emulating His example using his power or **means**, and imitating his love or **motivation**. In the case of Christ, his model, means, and motivation were always consistent. his model is always the Father. John 5:19 says, "So Jesus said to them, the Son can do nothing of his own accord, but only what he sees the Father doing. For whatever the Father does, that the Son does likewise."[40] The means is the power of the Holy Spirit rooted in love. Jesus was conceived to be human by the Holy Spirit (Luke 1:35), was led by the Holy Spirit (Luke 4:10), and resurrected by the Holy Spirit (Romans 8:11). The Apostle Paul explains the intended relationship between love and power in 1 Corinthians 13:2, where he says, "And if I have prophetic powers, and understand all mysteries and all knowledge, and if I have all faith, so as to remove mountains, but have not love, I am nothing."[41] The motivation is always to please or love the Father. Finally, Jesus in John 4:34 says, "My food is

---

[40] English Standard Version
[41] English Standard Version

to do the will of him who sent me and to accomplish his work."[42] So, let us delve deeper into these principles.

Model

As spouses, our model is always Christ. For husbands, we emulate Christ's love to the church. For wives, you emulate Christ's submission to the Father. I liken the process of marriage to putting together a puzzle. There are many pieces in the box, and it is a chore, and sometimes, a nightmare to fit the puzzle pieces where they belong. However, because the puzzle pieces will eventually replicate the larger picture on the box, it behooves the ones putting the puzzle together to frequently look at the model picture on the box. Similarly, we need to frequently look at the model of Christ as we endeavor to put the puzzle pieces of marriage together. The puzzle of our marriages will eventually portray the picture of Christ and his bride, the church. Husbands need to look intently at Christ's position towards His wife, and wives need to look intently at the position of the church in response to Christ.

Practically, this involves learning and being instructed in the wisdom of the Bible, especially those verses that give instruction regarding marriage. It means submitting to the

---

[42] English Standard Version

sanctifying work of the Holy Spirit. It means taking the love that Christ gave you and extending it toward your spouse. It means dying to our own selfish ways, so the picture of Christ can be easily seen. Our natural framework comes from our past experiences and sinful nature. What we know or think we know about marriage emanates from the marriages we have seen first-hand. If your parents were married, then what you saw and experienced in their marriage is most likely your greatest frame of reference. If your parents were not married, then the married couple you saw the most will likely be your greatest frame of reference. The problem with this reality is that, if the example was poor, we will replicate bad habits and have an improper view of marriage. If your parents' or grandparents' marriage was fair or even good, you still do not have the best example to have a great or excellent marriage. Consequently, Christ should be our example because he has loved and still loves his bride perfectly. Wives also have Jesus Christ as their model for he is the epitome of submission and trust. He not only submitted to his father in everything, but Christ trusted his father even at death. Jesus's final statement from the cross was "Father, into your hands I commit my spirit."[43] It does not matter how dysfunctional your human

[43] Luke 23:46 (English Standard Version)

examples may have been. We all have a perfect model to emulate and compare ourselves to.

Means

Our "means" is the Holy Spirit. The Holy Spirit gives us the power to do what is impossible for us to do naturally. Loving without the power of God is impossible. Forgiveness and faithfulness apart from the power of God is impossible. You can read hundreds of books, attend several workshops and conferences, but if you do not operate in your marriage by leaning on the power of God, your marriage will fail. To be clear, divorce is not the only way one's marriage can fail. Many couples who have miserable, dysfunctional, and fruitless marriages are failing in achieving God's intended purpose for marriage. Jesus, our model, depended on the power of God during his earthly journey. In every aspect of marriage, dependency on the Holy Spirit is necessary. Even as it pertains to submission, being led by the Spirit is a prerequisite to being able to submit. Hence, in Ephesians 5:18, Paul exhorts the believers in Ephesus to be filled with the Spirit. This exhortation occurs chronologically before the exhortation for husbands to love their wives as Christ loved the church and the exhortation for wives to submit to their own husbands as unto the Lord. In addition to the ability to submit,

God gives us the power to bear the fruits of the spirit: love, joy, peace, patience, kindness, goodness, faithfulness, gentleness, and self-control.[44] How do we access this power? The simplest response to that question is prayer! During impossible seasons and situations where nothing I did worked, I fell on my knees and prayed. God intervened and worked inside of me and outside of me to ameliorate the situation for good. We typically pray when a crisis arises. There is nothing wrong with praying while in a crisis. It is wiser, however, to pray all of the time, accessing the supernatural power to be victorious even when you and your marriage is not in crisis. The old adage says, "An ounce of prevention is worth a pound of cure." Be purposeful to pray fervently and often to empower your marriage.

Motivation

The motivation should always be to glorify God. Colossians 3:17 says, "And whatever you do, in word or deed, do everything in the name of the Lord Jesus, giving thanks to God the Father through him."[45] Jesus's primary motivation for doing what he did was to glorify his Father. When we pattern our motivations after Jesus, we cannot go wrong. This

---

[44] Galatians 5:22-23 (English Standard Version)
[45] English Standard Version

motivation to glorify God should be inspired by three things. First, the motive of our obedience and desire to glorify God should be based on a disposition of ***gratitude*** for how he loves us in spite of our failure to properly love him back. This attitude of gratitude should undergird our desire to please him. Second, the motivation to glorify God should be inspired by the reality of the ***judgment seat*** of Christ. Every Christian has to stand before the judgment seat of Christ and give an account of the deeds done in the body whether the deeds are good or bad (2 Corinthians 5:9-10). Part of what motivates me to be a loving and godly husband is that I will eventually be judged for my performance. I want God to say, "Well done!" Thirdly, our motivation should be inspired by the opportunity to be a ***positive example*** for others, especially people over whom we have direct influence. Specifically, the audience that will, most often, be influenced the most by your marriage is your spouse and your children. How spouses relate to one another creates the human framework for how their children will relate in their future relationships. Extending out from the family into the neighborhood or workplaces, spouses can have a tremendous evangelistic impact on people who struggle to experience the love of Christ in their lives. If our motive is only to love ourselves, then the marriage will not thrive.

Biblical Passages for Reflection

Ephesians 5:1-2

Ephesians 5:17-18

Ephesians 5:22-31

John 13:34-35

Summary Principles:

1) Jesus is our model for love, respect, and submission in our marriage.

2) The Holy Spirit is the means (power) that enables us to love, respect, forgive, and submit within our marriage.

3) Our deepest motive for what we do in the marriage should be to glorify God. That was the motive Jesus had in everything he did.

Simplified Marriage Exhortation:

Love your spouse as Christ loved his father and the church!

Prayer:

Father, I pray that you would guide my vision to see the example of Jesus. He is the perfect spouse and example to emulate. Help develop my prayer life so I may obtain supernatural power to love my spouse as Christ loved me. Let my deepest motive be to glorify you. In Jesus's name, Amen.

Journal

Who have you modeled your marriage after the most? What is your deepest motive for your decisions in the marriage or engagement?

Chapter 6

Covenant Love

I will betroth you to me forever. I will betroth you to me in righteousness and in justice, in steadfast love, and in mercy. I will betroth you to me in faithfulness. And you shall know the LORD.[46]

MICHAEL AND REBEKAH came to my office seeking pre-marital counseling. During the session, I asked Michael, "Why do you love Rebekah?" He replied, "I love Becca because of how she treats me. She accepts me for who I am, she is always there for me, she is kind to me, and picks me up

[46] Hosea 2:19-20 (English Standard Version)

when I am feeling low." Now, many people would say, "Awww that is so sweet. Yes, he really loves her." Well, in reality, Michael did not answer my question. I did not ask him **how Rebekah loves him**; rather, I asked him **why he loves her**. Michael had not conceptualized love from the perspective of denying self for the benefit of others. He, like so many of us, conceptualized love from the perspective of "what do I get out of it?" Herein lies the problem of love -- many people do not really know what it is. The word is used so frequently that the pure essence of what it is and how it ought to be displayed has been diluted from our culture. The type of love that is required in holy and healthy marriages is agape love. Agape love, as mentioned earlier, is the godly, selfless love that denies self for the best interest of others. Many people are confused about what agape love looks like. In this chapter, I will give descriptions of what agape love is and what it is not. I will also write about how the love between spouses should be undergirded by their covenant vow to God and to each other. First, let us endeavor to discuss what agape love is not. On the following page, I list some of the most common misconceptions about love.

Misconceptions about Love

1) Love is an emotion.

2) Love is reciprocal

3) You can fall in and out of love

4) Love is an adjective

5) You can love without God

1) Love is an emotion

Many people are driven by an emotional experience to speak these three words, "I love you." Their profession of love is based on how they feel. This is not love. Instead, it is whatever emotion you are feeling at the time. The difficulty of loving strictly based on emotion is that emotions change. What happens when you do not feel the same? Most marriages start off well. Both spouses are emotionally happy and expectant of a blissful marriage. When the thrill of marriage wears off and the reality of the magnitude of problems sets in, emotions quickly change from happy to irritable. When trauma enters the marriage because of infidelity, abuse, sickness, or other factors, this "emotional love" becomes impossible to sustain. This is because emotional love does not have a sure foundation. Its foundation changes like the tide. On the other hand, real love has a sure foundation that does not change despite the devastation of life's storms.

Many persons, whether currently married or preparing to be married, have the belief that marriage is supposed to "50-50." Some people are so technical about this principle that they divide all of the bills, the chores, and the responsibilities completely down the middle. This philosophy of marriage being 50-50 is more in line with a *Business* model of partnership rather than a *Biblical* one. In the business model, the goal is to invest as little as possible and gain as much as possible. The Biblical model is just the opposite. God wants us to give as much as we can without expecting anything in return, except for him to be glorified. Jesus points out this principle when he tells his disciples that whoever saves his life will lose it; however, whoever loses his life for his sake will save it.[47] Jesus, being the perfect personification of love, demonstrated this when he loved his bride enough to die for her. Jesus did not emotionally "feel" like dying. In fact, he requested in the Garden of Gethsemane that his Father "remove the cup." The Bible declares that Jesus was

[47] Matthew 16:25 (English Standard Version)

sorrowful unto death. If Jesus based his decision to die on his emotions, he would not have done it. However, his decision was motivated by something stronger. The love that Jesus had for the Father manifested itself in a commitment to suffer a violent and vicarious death so that his bride -- the church could have eternal life.

2) Love is reciprocal

I see this misconception play out frequently in marriage counseling. Often, spouses come in for marriage counseling and give their resume about how strong their love has been, how many sacrifices have been made, how much harm they have had to endure, and how long they have waited for reciprocation. The problem is that love does not need *reciprocation,* it needs *expression.* The fulfillment of love is not in what it receives in return, but in what it gives. The most tangible demonstration we have of love is when Jesus died on the cross for sinners who rejected him. This decision was a one-way gift to people who did not fully understand how awesome this gift was when it was rendered. Modeling this type of agape love is challenging in many marriages. The constant sacrificing seems unnatural, and it is difficult not to expect reciprocity. Many spouses are motivated by what they are going to get in return. When they do not receive the compensation at the rate or the way they were expecting it, they become bitter and resentful. In the midst of their bitterness and grudge-holding, they slowly begin to take away the things they were once doing "in the name of love." That behavior really is not love. It is a calculated investment which seeks to yield beneficial returns. The love that Jesus poured out on the cross, however, still speaks. It reminds us of what real love costs. Furthermore, Jesus said in Acts 20:35, "It is more blessed to give than to receive."[48] Joy is maximized in the giving and not the receiving. Wow! What a deep revelation! Please internalize this revelation. Real love is not about you. It is about you giving and sacrificing of yourself to meet the needs of someone else.

3) You can fall in and out of love

The phrase *falling in love* sounds poetically beautiful, but it is utterly misleading. A popular reason why couples divorce is that one of the spouses "fell out of love" or he/she was not "in love" anymore. Falling in and/or out of love implies a temporary state that is subject to change based on the unpredictable events of life. Love is the strongest power on the planet. It, therefore, has the power to weather any storm no matter how devastating and no matter how long the storm

---

[48] English Standard Version

lasts. The problem is not in love's ability; rather the problem is in our refusal to understand, receive, and ultimately give true love. The terminology "in love" is actually accurate if the person you are in love with is Jesus Christ. Every Christian is positioned "in Christ." Consequently, every Christian, while being "in Christ," has Christ "in them." Christ living in the Christian is a permanent and eternal reality. The Apostle Paul says that we are sealed with the promised Holy Spirit, who is the guarantee of our inheritance.[49] In other words, the moment we come to Christ by faith, he seals us permanently and gives us the promise of his eternal love. Love is a permanent state. God promises never to leave us nor forsake us. The apostle Paul goes on to assure Christians that nothing could separate them from the love of God.[50] Therefore, when people claim that they fell out of love with someone, they never really fully loved the person in the first place. It is a cop out to avoid real commitment.

4.) Love is an adjective

Love is an **action word**! True love is evidenced by behavior. We have been so conditioned to be aroused by the profession of love, we do not look for the behavior of love.

[49] Ephesians 1:13-14 (portions) English Standard Version
[50] Romans 8:35-39

The Apostle John, speaking tenderly to his audience says, "Little children, let us not love in word or talk but in deed and in truth."[51] In other words, do less talking the talk and more walking the walk. Furthermore, in the most popular chapter of love in the Bible (1 Corinthians 13), the Apostle Paul uses many action words to describe love. In the English translations of verses 4-5, the key words appear to be adjectives. For example, "Love is patient and kind; love does not envy or boast; it is not arrogant or rude. It does not insist on its own way; it is not irritable or resentful."[52] In the original Greek rendering, however, the words are better translated as verbs, not adjectives. There are sixteen action verbs in verses 4-8 that describe the activity of love:

1) Love suffers long

2) Love acts kindly

3) Love does not envy (Love acts contently)[53]

4) Love does not boast (Love acts modestly)

[51] 1 John 3:18 (English Standard Version)
[52] English Standard Version
[53] Author's affirmative synonyms in parentheses (#3-10;16)

5) Love does not act conceitedly (Love acts meekly

6) Love does not behave rudely (Love acts politely)

7) Love does not insist on its own way (Love yields)

8) Love does not allow itself to be resentful (Love forgives)

9) Love does not think of evil (Love focuses on good)

10) Love does not rejoice at wrongdoing (Love rejoices at what is right)

11) Love rejoices with the truth

12) Love bears all things

13) Love believes all things

14) Love hopes all things

15) Love endures all things

16) Love never ends (Love acts always)

These verses speak to the unequivocal truth that **Love is an action!**

5) You can love without God

The same way modern culture has taken Christ out of Christmas, it has almost succeeded in taking God out of love. Valentine's Day, is referred to as "Love Day." The marketing efforts from Hallmark, Dove, FTD, and other companies are largely successful because God is not used in the marketing. Can you imagine a Valentine's Day card with a cross and blood emanating from the wood? The world wants to sell love without God, but it is impossible to love without God for God is love. Without God, the capacity to love is nonexistent. 1 John 4:7-8 says,

> *Beloved, let us love one another for love is from God, and whoever loves has been born of God and knows God. Anyone who does not love does not know God, because God is love.*[54]

The Pleasures of Covenant Love

As mentioned in chapter one, joy and pleasure are secondary purposes of marriage. God's love for his children includes provisions of joy and pleasure. A good example of this is the Garden of Eden. Before Adam and Eve forfeited

[54] English Standard Version

their paradise, God had designed a reality where all of their needs and desires were met. The caveat was God's will had to be the priority. As long as that was the case, joy and pleasures abounded. Similarly, when spouses prioritize God's glory in their marriage, they can experience great happiness and pleasure. Below is a short, non-exhaustive list of some specific pleasures in a loving marriage.

1) Sexual Pleasure
2) Companionship
3) Partnership

Sexual Pleasure

As discussed earlier, God designed sex to be used only in the context of marriage. Many people experience sexual pleasure outside of marriage, but that pleasure does not compare to the pleasure derived from sharing sexual intimacy with one's covenant love. Additionally, immoral sexual relations come with emotional, physical, financial, and spiritual consequences. In the context of marriage, the sexual relationship is holy and without guilt or shame. Proverbs 5 states,

> *Drink water from your own cistern, flowing water from your own well. Should your springs be scattered abroad, streams of water in the street? Let them be for yourself alone, and not for strangers with you. Let your fountain be blessed, and rejoice in the wife of your youth, a lovely deer, a graceful doe. Let her breasts fill you at all times with delight; be intoxicated always in her love.*[55]

Companionship

God did not create humans as islands unto themselves. He created us for community. He created us to share socially in fellowship. I contend that my best companion, next to God, is my wife. Many people say their best companion is their pet. The common adage is "a dog is man's best friend." A dog will not tell me things that make me better. A spouse's companionship or loyal friendship grows deeper throughout the marriage and is a cistern full of love and support.

Partnership

Ecclesiastes 4 states,

> *Two are better than one, because they have a good reward for their toil. For if they fall, one will lift up his fellow. But woe to him who is alone when he falls and has not another to lift*

---

[55] Proverbs 5:15-19 (English Standard Version)

> *him up! Again, if two lie together, they keep warm, but how can one keep warm alone? And though a man might prevail against one who is alone, two will withstand him—a threefold cord is not quickly broken*[56]

Husbands and wives should be partners in every sense of the word. They should be partners in covenant love, in ministry, in business matter, in parenting, in sex, and in mutual sanctification. What a benefit to have a spouse that supports you and stands by and with you even during difficult seasons. As the above scripture states, two is better than one. Even if at present time your marriage is not operating in healthy partnership, the potential for improvement exists, especially if there is *Hesed* or steadfast love in the marriage.

Hesed or *Chesed* is a Hebrew word found numerous times in the Old Testament of the Bible. It has been translated to mean mercy, lovingkindness, loyal love, and steadfast love. All of these words that describe the *chesed* of God are connected to the concept and reality of covenant. God is a covenant-keeper, and his covenant with Israel was a commitment that would not be broken, even when Israel broke the terms of the agreement. This commitment required God

[56] Ecclesiastes 4:9-12 (English Standard Version)

to be merciful, patient, kind, and loyal to the vow that he made without ceasing.

Psalm 89 poignantly describes God's covenant promise regarding King David,

> *My steadfast love I will keep for him forever, and my covenant will stand firm for him. I will establish his offspring forever and his throne as the days of the heavens. If his children forsake my law and do not walk according to my rules, if they violate my statutes and do not keep my commandments, then I will punish their transgression with the rod and their iniquity with stipes, but I will not remove from him my steadfast love or be false to my faithfulness. I will not violate my covenant or alter the word that went forth from my lips*[57]

In that psalm, God is making a covenant with David, and God promises that nothing will make him disavow His word. Similarly, when a man and woman enter into holy matrimony, they are entering into a covenant. The covenant is undoubtedly with their spouse; however, it is also with God. In fact, the covenant with God should supersede the covenant with one's spouse. For example, the marital covenant is predicated on the practice of "forsaking all others." Consequently, if one spouse is unfaithful and has sex with

[57] English Standard Version

someone else, he/she has violated an aspect of the covenant arrangement. Once the offended party is privy to the infidelity, he/she has no reason to continue the marital covenant unless he/she is bound by another covenant. This other covenant is the one made to God. This is a hard pill to swallow. Let me be clear, infidelity is such a no-no and it should be. Many couples enter into marriage with their minds made up that infidelity is a deal-breaker for the marriage. If that were God's position, however, then none of us would be here. God's *chesed* toward us allows him to be loyal to us and to his vow even when we violate the terms of our vow to him. This truth about God's steadfast love toward us is not a license for couples to be unfaithful; rather, it is an opportunity to love and forgive each other in spite of seemingly unforgivable offenses. This leads us to the last chapter in this book--forgiveness.

Biblical Passages for Reflection

Hosea 2:14-20

1 John 4:7-8

1 Corinthians 13:1-13

1 John 3:16-18

Summary Principles:

1) Misconceptions of agape love include

    - Love is an emotion
    - Love is reciprocal
    - You can fall in and out of love
    - Love is an adjective
    - You can love without God

2) Real love (agape) is selfless and has the best interest of others in mind.

3) The vows one made to God regarding one's marriage should supersede the vows made to one's spouse.

4) *Hesed* describes God's steadfast love in the context of a covenant. *Hesed* or covenant loyalty requires or leads to mercy and forgiveness for very painful offenses within the marriage.

Simplified and Sanctified Exhortation:

Keep the vow you made before God and before your spouse! Love your spouse with agape love!

Prayer:

Father, please empower me to be steadfast and loyal like you and keep the vows I made to you and to my spouse. Even if my spouse does me wrong, I will continue to do right by you. In Jesus's name, Amen.

Journal

What are the deal breakers in your marriage or engagement? Can your covenantal vow overcome them?

Chapter 7

Faithful Forgiveness

Then Peter came up and said to him, "Lord, how often will my brother sin against me, and I forgive him? As many as seven times?" Jesus said to him, "I do not say to you seven times, but seventy times seven."[58]

DENNIS IS THE founder and CEO of a large construction company. His company has over 150 employees and his revenues exceed $25 million annually. Dennis is a visionary. When he developed the business plan years ago, Dennis envisioned that his business would earn millions of

[58] Matthew 18:21-22 (English Standard Version)

dollars in revenue. Through countless meetings with the board, coaching sessions with upper management, and long hours at work, Dennis is living his dream. Well, sort of. One of the other staples of Dennis's dream was that his family would live comfortably and he would be able to leave a legacy to his three daughters and one son. Unfortunately, the legacy that Dennis left his family was bitterness. His wife filed for divorce due to infidelity. Dennis did not commit adultery with another woman; however, he slept with his business. Many nights he literally slept in his office and did not come home. Although Dennis has received numerous awards for his business success, he seldom was celebrated by his wife and children.

Healthy marriages hinge on the practice of faithful forgiveness. The only way Dennis's wife can reconsider her trajectory towards divorce is with the decision to forgive the cumulative offenses of her husband. Dennis undoubtedly needs to repent, beg for mercy, and radically allow God to transform his priorities; however, this does not guarantee forgiveness and reconciliation. The truth of the matter is that Dennis does not deserve to be forgiven nor to be reconciled with his wife. The good news is that forgiveness does not require that. Forgiveness is a gift that is neither earned nor deserved. It is an expression of grace and mercy. Without consistent and faithful forgiveness in one's marriage, the marriage is doomed to fail.

I contend that the greatest culprit of unhappy marriages, separations, and divorces is unforgiveness. Let me state unequivocally that forgiveness does not mean that the offended party fails to confront and indict the offender and "just get over it;" rather, the offended spouse seeks to forgive faithfully and consistently. Unfortunately, many spouses let the offense linger on by holding on to bitterness and refusing to forgive. Without faithful forgiveness, however, the marriage relationship will eventually be filled with hurt, insensitivity, selfishness, neglect, unhealthy priorities, betrayal, and misunderstandings. There is no conceivable way that a husband and wife can hurt each other frequently (whether intentionally or unintentionally), and continue to thrive unless there is the constant practice of forgiveness. Here are the top four reasons in order of importance why spouses should forgive.

1) Forgiveness glorifies God

God is glorified when we forgive. God is glorified when we respond obediently to his commands. Because God is a forgiving God, when we act like he acts, we reflect his nature on the earth.

2) Forgiveness is an expression of love

In John 13:34-35, Jesus says, "A new commandment I give to you, that you love one another: just as I have loved you, you are also to love one another."[59] One of the primary ways Jesus demonstrated his love for us is by forgiving us. Specifically, his sacrifice on the cross was efficacious enough to forgive our past sins, present sins, and even future sins. Spouses can demonstrate love in marriage by regularly and consistently forgiving each other. A spouse who claims to love his/her spouse but refuses to forgive is not actively loving his/her spouse.

3) Forgiveness unifies the relationship

Apostle Paul explains in 2 Corinthians 2:11 that unforgiveness in our relationships allows Satan to "outwit" us.[60] Specifically, Satan takes the unforgiveness between parties and causes even more division in the relationship. This is why Paul encourages Christians to be angry without sinning and to not to let the sun go down on their anger.[61] These two verses were written in the specific context of being members of the same church fellowship body. We can apply these

---

[59] English Standard Version
[60] English Standard Version
[61] Ephesians 4:26 (English Standard Version)

truths to marriage as husbands and wives are also members of the same body. Here is the point, when there is unforgiveness, there is division. Satan uses the division to pull apart the relationship. Many married couples can attest to the fact that some arguments that lasted for weeks or months began with a tiny disagreement. That tiny disagreement morphed into a gaping hole of division. When forgiveness is swift and consistent, it reestablishes the unity in the marriage relationship.

4) Forgiveness benefits spouses holistically

Many health studies over the years have found a correlation between unforgiveness and certain diseases. In particular, some studies found a correlation between unforgiveness and heart disease. Other studies point to the correlation between unforgiveness and cancer. Some studies detail the correlation between unforgiveness and chronic anxiety and even depression.

Forgiveness not only benefits spouses physically and psychologically, but spiritually as well. Spiritually speaking, unforgiveness allows Satan to have greater influence in our lives which undoubtedly turns us away from God. The reason why we can forgive is because Christ first forgave us. When we meditate on how God graciously and mercifully forgave us when our sins were unforgivable, it should inspire us to forgive those who have harmed us. When spouses remember that they are recipients of God's forgiveness and forgive faithfully, the power of God is working mightily within them. Overflowing peace, health, and joy emanate from a decision to faithfully practice forgiveness.

Misconceptions regarding forgiveness[62]

Just as there are common misconceptions about love, there are misconceptions about forgiveness that need to be clarified.

1) Everyone can forgive

Forgiveness is not a function of our fallen human nature. God must empower us to forgive because forgiveness is antithetical to our natural instinct to protect ourselves.

---

[62] More detailed information about forgiveness is in my book, ***The Forgiveness Diet***

2) Forgiveness is the same as reconciliation

Many people confuse forgiveness and reconciliation. Forgiveness is the releasing of a debt. Reconciliation is the process of the two reuniting as one. Forgiveness should precede reconciliation; however, reconciliation should also be dependent on character change. In the example of Dennis, his wife should forgive him and not pursue the divorce. She should forgive him because that is God's will. She should not pursue divorce because Dennis's poor prioritization of his wife is not a Biblical reason for divorce. However, Dennis needs to repent and change before true reconciliation can take place. Is it possible to forgive and not reconcile? Yes, it is possible but not optimal. God gives all Christians the ministry of reconciliation. However, reconciliation involves agreement by both parties. There may be seasons where one party has forgiven the other party, but the other party has not repented nor expressed a sincere interest in reconciling. Within the context of marriage, reconciliation is always the goal. Hence, spouses should forgive each other and wait for the other spouse to repent and humbly seek reconciliation.

3) It is easy to forgive and forget

People are often encouraged to forgive and forget. The reality is that forgiveness does not cause one to forget the offense; rather, it is a decision not to hold the offender responsible for the offense. This results in a progressive reduction of hurt and bitterness until the pain is completely gone. While the forgiver seeks to cast the memory as far away from his/her mind, it will be triggered periodically. When the memory of the offense is triggered, peace should be experienced as the forgiver remembers that the offense has been pardoned.

4) Everyone is entitled to be forgiven

Some people (spouses) have a sense of entitlement where they demand to be forgiven. Such a demand is misplaced as the offender has no right or "legal entitlement" to make such a "demand." Forgiveness is a gracious and merciful gift. The forgiver will only forgive at the moment when he/she is ready and able. This reality has major implications for married couples as many offenders seek to put pressure on their spouses to forgive and move on. The offending party should be humble, penitent, and patient, and wait for the gift of forgiveness.

The reality of marriage is that spouses offend each other on a daily basis. Some of the offenses are intentional and premeditated, while others are accidental and unintentional. Harm is still harm and pain is still pain. Forgiveness allows couples to deal with the offense not by ignoring it, but resolving it by letting it go. When this forgiveness process occurs in marriage faithfully and consistently, reconciliation and fruitfulness will increase. Remember, do not forgive because your spouse deserves it; rather forgive because God commands you do to so. The secret to having a simplified and sanctified marriage is to **Love God and Keep His Commandments.**

Biblical Passages for Reflection

Matthew 18:21-35

Ephesians 4:25-32

2 Corinthians 2:5-11

Matthew 6:5-14

Summary Principles:

We should forgive because:

1) Forgiveness glorifies God
2) Forgiveness is an expression of love
3) Forgiveness unifies the marriage/community
4) Forgiveness benefits the forgiver holistically.

Simplified and Sanctified Exhortation:

Forgive your spouse faithfully as an act of obedience to God.

Prayer:

Father, please help me to forgive as you have forgiven me. I understand that forgiveness is a gift and that it is underserved. Help me to forgive when I do not feel like it. Help me always to remember how you constantly forgive me. I need your supernatural ability to help me forgive my spouse for the many hurts in my marriage. In Jesus's name, Amen.

Journal

Do you struggle with unforgiveness? How long does it take you to forgive offenses? How has unforgiveness affected the peace and unity of your marriage?

Final Thoughts

I am grateful that God has providentially led you to read this book. I pray you were blessed, encouraged, and edified. I would not trade my journey in marriage for the world. As God has simplified my understanding of marriage, I have allowed him to sanctify me more willingly. Wherever you are on your marital journey, please be encouraged that it will get better as you adhere to the blueprint. May God bless you and your marriage!

Dr. Jendayo Grady

Askdrgrady.com

@askdrgrady

301-699-2169

drjendayogrady@gmail.com

Other resources by Dr. Jendayo Grady

The Forgiveness Diet: How to Lose the Weight and Keep it Off

https://www.amazon.com/Forgiveness-Diet-Lose-Weight-Keep/dp/1432764942/ref=sr_1_2_twi_pap_3?ie=UTF8&qid=1472441288&sr=8-2&keywords=the+forgiveness+diet

www.ingramcontent.com/pod-product-compliance
Lightning Source LLC
Chambersburg PA
CBHW031856090426
42741CB00005B/516